Slam Dunk Dilemma!

Maverick
Chapter Readers

'Slam Dunk Dilemma!'
An original concept by Jenny Moore
© Jenny Moore

Illustrated by Ellie Oshea

Published by MAVERICK ARTS PUBLISHING LTD
Studio 11, City Business Centre, 6 Brighton Road,
Horsham, West Sussex, RH13 5BB
© Maverick Arts Publishing Limited February 2021
+44 (0)1403 256941

A CIP catalogue record for this book is available at the British Library.

ISBN 978-1-84886-784-0

www.maverickbooks.co.uk

This book is rated as: Brown Band (Guided Reading)

Slam Dunk Dilemma!

Written by **Jenny Moore**

Illustrated by **Ellie Oshea**

Chapter 1

Zac stared at the pencil height marks on the kitchen doorframe. It had been weeks since Mum last measured him, marking the line with her pencil to show how much he'd grown. But Zac *wasn't* growing. That was the problem. The line had barely moved since Christmas. His big brother Cam seemed to shoot up another inch every month, yet Zac was still as short as ever.

Cam was lucky. He was even taller than Mum now. It made shooting hoops in basketball so much easier.

Cam could jump all the way up to the net and push the ball through, in the perfect slam dunk.

If only Zac could hurry up and grow before his school basketball match on Thursday. He'd been doing special stretching exercises every morning to try and speed things up. He'd been eating boiled eggs and wholegrain toast for breakfast, plus extra vegetables with each meal. He'd drunk a whole pint of milk every day. But had it worked? Had he got any taller? There was only one way to find out.

"Please can you do the pencil mark for me?" he asked Cam. Zac pressed himself against the doorframe and pulled back his shoulders, thinking tall thoughts. But it was no good.

"You're still the same height as last time," said Cam, as Zac twisted round to see.

Zac spiked up his hair and stood on tiptoe. "What about now?"

Cam laughed. "That's cheating! Cheer up," he added, "I wasn't very tall when I was your age. I'm sure you'll grow soon."

"I need to grow *now*," said Zac, glumly. "It's only two days until our big match."

"You don't have to be tall to be good at basketball," Cam told him, bouncing an imaginary ball and pretending to score. "You've been practising so hard, I'm sure you'll be brilliant. Just do your best and have fun."

Zac knew Cam was only trying to help, but his heart sank as he thought about all that extra practice going to waste. What chance did he have against the other team if he couldn't reach as high as them?

Chapter 2

Zac was still feeling gloomy as he walked home from school the next day. He stopped outside the charity shop at the end of his road, checking his reflection in the window. No. He still didn't look any taller.

But then something else caught his eye... a pair of trainers. They weren't just any old trainers though, Zac realised as he peered through the glass. They were special Ultra Bounce shoes, like the ones in Cam's basketball magazine.

Hmm, he thought. He couldn't make himself any taller but perhaps the shoes would help him jump higher. It was worth a try. Zac raced back home and emptied out his piggy bank. He arranged the coins into neat piles on his bedroom floor and counted them up. NO! He was still a whole pound short!

"Hey, Cam," he called, rushing downstairs to find his brother. Cam was stretched out on the sofa, reading his latest magazine. "Can you lend me some money? I need another pound. Please," he begged. "It's an emergency."

Cam shook his head. "Sorry, I've already spent my pocket money this week. We could try checking under the furniture though. Sometimes coins fall out of Mum's jeans!"

Cam rolled off the sofa to have a look but he couldn't get down low enough to see. He was too tall. His bottom kept bumping into the coffee table.

"Let me try," said Zac, slipping down into the space with no trouble at all. Sometimes being short had its advantages.

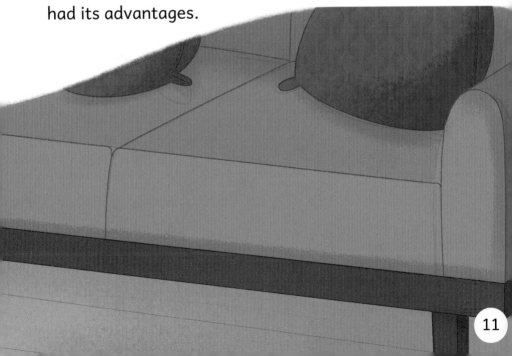

"There are *loads* of things down here... let me see if I can reach..."

His fingers closed round something small and round. Zac pulled it out for a closer look. "Ugh, yuck!" It was a shrivelled slice of carrot.

"How did *that* get under there?" He tried again, pulling out one useless item after another. He found a sweet wrapper, a dead spider, a penny, and two dirty tissues.

"Double yuck!"

Zac tried one last time,

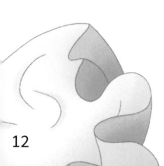

squeezing his arm all the way to the back. There was definitely something else there. Something flat and hard and round...

"Yes!" It was a pound coin! Zac punched the air in excitement. It was a bit sticky, but he didn't care about that. He wiped it on his shorts and tucked it into his pocket along with the rest of his money. "Thanks Cam. That was a great idea!"

Zac hurried back to the charity shop, hoping the shoes were still there.

Chapter 3

Zac peered in through the shop window. He was in luck. There they were!

The Ultra Bounce shoes looked even better than he'd remembered. They were bright red, with yellow laces and thick bouncy soles. But would they fit him? Zac crossed his fingers and went in.

"Hello," said the lady behind the counter. "Can I help you?"

"I'd like to try the shoes in the window, please," Zac told her. "The special bouncy red ones."

"Oh yes," said the lady as she fetched them for him. "These shoes are very bouncy. In fact they were *too* bouncy for the girl who brought them in. She only wore them once!"

Zac sat down on a pink unicorn stool and swapped his scruffy old trainers for the Ultra Bounce shoes.

They were the perfect fit.

He did up the laces and took a test walk round the shop. They really *were* bouncy.

He tried out a proper jump, reaching up with his fingers as if he was shooting for the net.

BOING!

Zac jumped so high his fingers touched the ceiling!

"Wow," he told the shop lady. "These shoes are amazing. I'll take them!"

"Thank you," said the lady as Zac handed over the money. "I hope you enjoy wearing them."

"Thanks," replied Zac with a big grin. "I'm going to try them out in my school basketball match tomorrow. I can't wait!"

Chapter 4

It's only a game, Zac told himself as he sat in the changing room. It was an important game though. If his team won this match, they'd be through to the semi-finals. How cool would that be?

Zac slipped on his Ultra Bounce shoes, tying the laces with a double bow to make sure they stayed tight.

"Come on, you can do this," he said out loud, trying to make himself feel better. Perhaps a few warm-up jumps would help.

BOING!

Woah! Zac had forgotten just how springy his new shoes were! His nerves faded away as he jumped higher and higher. Soon he was raring to go.

"Cool shoes," said his teammates as they headed onto the court.

"Very cool," agreed his basketball coach, Mrs Hoop.

"Thanks." Zac looked down at his feet and smiled. "Wait until you see how bouncy they are. I'm going to score loads of points with these on."

The referee threw the ball up into the air and the game began. They were off!

Zac was buzzing with energy and excitement now. His feet had never felt lighter!

BOING... He leapt sideways to seize control of the ball.

SWERVE... He dived to the left, bouncing as he went. But someone else was coming in from the other side now. He swung back round to the right.

Come on shoes!

BOING, BOING... The net was right there, waiting for him to shoot. He reached up and...

Yes! Slam dunk! Two points!

Zac did a giant leap to celebrate, punching the air

with his fist. Mrs Hoop cheered from the sideline.

BOING...

Shoot...

Two points!

BOING, BOING, BOING...

Shoot...

Three points!

Zac scored point after point. There was no stopping him!

"Nice work, everyone," said Mrs Hoop at half time. "And *very* well done to you, Zac," she added. "Those shots were amazing. It must be those new magic shoes of yours!"

"Yes," agreed Zac. "It must be."

The second half of the match went even better. Zac had never scored so many points in his life. He'd never jumped so high. But it wasn't as much fun this time. Mrs Hoop's words kept coming back to him. *It must be those magic shoes of yours.*

What if they really *were* magic? That wouldn't be very fair on the other team, would it? It felt a bit like cheating. In fact, it felt a *lot* like cheating.

Everyone crowded round Zac at the end of the match, slapping him on the back and high-fiving him.

"You're a legend!" they said. "What a star!"

But Zac didn't feel like a star. He felt like a fake.

It wasn't me, he thought miserably. *It was my shoes.* He ran back to the changing room and tugged them off, without even stopping to untie the laces. Then he stuffed them down the bottom of his kit bag so he wouldn't be tempted to cheat with them again. His scruffy old trainers would have to do from now on.

Chapter 5

It was semi-finals day.

Zac should have been excited but he was too busy thinking about the magic shoes waiting at the bottom of his kit bag.

"It's a good job we've got you on our side," his friends said as they filed into the changing room. "Have you seen the other team? They're like giants!"

Zac nodded. He knew all about the Flintmouth Academy team from Cam. They'd won the county school cup every year for the past ten years.

"They are pretty tall," he agreed. "We'll just have to jump higher, won't we?" he added, tying the laces on his old trainers.

Zac's feet felt heavy and clumsy as he headed out onto the court. The Flintmouth Academy players looked even bigger close up.

Would he still be able to reach the net without his
Ultra Bounce shoes?

The first half of the game went terribly. Zac missed
every single shot and his passes were all over the
place. He wasn't a match hero this time, he was a
match loser.

"Come on, Zac," called Mrs Hoop. "You can do it."

But Zac *couldn't* do it—not without his new shoes.

He tore back to the changing room at half-time and rescued the Ultra Bounce shoes from the bottom of his bag. This was an emergency. He kicked off his old trainers, swapping them for his new ones. There! That was better.

Zac's feet felt lighter and bouncier already, but his heart felt heavier than ever as he bounded back onto court for the second half.

That's cheating, said a little voice inside his head. Zac shook the thought away again and got back to the game. He was back on winning form now, bouncing super-high and scoring lots of points.

By the end of the match the teams were drawing. There were only seconds to go as Zac bent his knees

and sprung towards the basket, shooting as he went.

"YES!"

His teammates went wild as the ball dropped through the net and the final whistle blew. "Well done, Zac!" called Mrs Hoop. "You did it!"

No. It wasn't me, thought Zac. *It was my shoes.*

Chapter 6

Mum had made pizzas for dinner that night, to celebrate Zac's team reaching the finals. She'd loaded them up with all his favourite toppings and extra cheese on top. But Zac wasn't in the mood for celebration. He was still thinking about the match. It was the magic shoes that deserved a treat for winning the game, not him.

"What's wrong?" asked Cam, helping himself to a fifth slice of pizza. "You've hardly eaten anything."

"I'm not very hungry," Zac said quietly.

"Not very hungry?" repeated Cam. "But homemade pizzas are your favourite!"

"I don't deserve a special meal," Zac explained. "The only reason I scored all those points in the second half was because I was wearing my Ultra Bounce shoes. I was terrible in the first half without them. They're the ones that should get pizza, not me."

Zac half-expected Cam to laugh at the idea of pizza-eating trainers. It did sound a bit silly when he said it out loud. But his brother just smiled. "Special hoop-shooting shoes?" asked Cam. "They sound brilliant! I've got a secret weapon of my own, to help me aim better," he admitted. "It's my lucky wristband." He pulled a yellow wristband out of his pocket to show Zac. "A bit of extra luck always comes in handy."

"Wow. Does it work?" asked Zac, feeling better already.

"I keep scoring, so I guess it must do." Cam winked. "Why don't you try it for yourself? You can borrow it for the finals next week."

"Really? Do you mean it?" Zac slipped it onto his wrist.

"Of course," said Cam. "That's what brothers are for. Now hurry up and eat some more pizza before it's all gone!"

Chapter 7

It was the day of the big basketball final against Parkwell School. Zac took his Ultra Bounce shoes out of his kit bag and stuffed them under his bed before he left. That way he couldn't change his mind halfway through the game. "No magic shoes for me today," he promised himself.

By the time the school minibus drew up outside Parkwell School that afternoon, Zac's stomach was knotted with nerves. Had he done the right thing? How would he manage without his secret weapon?

But then he remembered his brother's lucky wristband. As soon as Zac put it on he felt better. He might not be able to bounce so high without his shoes, but at least his aim would be good now.

"Good luck, everyone," said Mrs Hoop. "I'm so proud of you all for reaching the final. Whatever happens today, you're all winners to me."

Zac felt a fresh rush of determination. "Thanks, Mrs Hoop. We'll do our best."

His old trainers were much less bouncy but Zac put extra energy into every jump to make up for it.

BOING... Zac passed the ball to Lee in time for him to make the perfect shot.

Yes! Two points!

Ravi was clear now. Zac aimed the ball between two members of the other team.

ZOOM! The ball flew through the gap, straight into Ravi's waiting hands. Ravi took a shot and...

Yes! Another two points! Thanks to Cam's lucky wristband, Zac's aim was better than ever...

Two more points!

Three points!

And again!

By the time Zac scored the winning basket, Mrs

Hoop was leaping up and down in celebration.

Zac and his friends were bursting with excitement as the final whistle blew. They'd done it! They were the champions! Zac felt super proud of himself for playing so well, without any help from his magic shoes. But he did have help from Cam's wristband though. His heart sank again. What if *that* was a kind of cheating too?

Chapter 8

"Are we having pizzas again to celebrate?" asked Zac.

Cam shook his head. "No, even better," he said. "Mum's taking us to Slam Dunk for dinner!"

The Slam Dunk Diner was Zac and Cam's favourite place to eat in the whole world. Everything about it was basketball-themed, from the round orange napkins to the hoop lights on the walls. They even had court markings painted on the ceiling!

"I'm going to have chicken dunkers," said Cam. "With extra onion hoops and a double dribble of barbecue sauce. And a side order of salad," he added, to keep Mum happy. "What about you Zac?"

"I don't know..." Zac shook his head. "My stomach feels a bit funny."

"You're not still worrying about those shoes, are you?" asked Cam. "You didn't even wear them this time."

"No," admitted Zac. "But I did wear your lucky wristband. What if that's the only reason we won?"

Cam laughed. "There's nothing lucky about that band, Zac. It's just an old one I found in my pocket."

Zac was confused. "But you said it helped you with your aim."

"I was trying to make you feel better," explained Cam. "I thought a lucky wristband might stop you worrying about your shoes."

"It *was* lucky though." Zac pulled the band off his wrist and held it up. "My aim was perfect when I was wearing it."

"The only thing that wristband gave you was extra confidence," said Cam. "Your aim was better because you believed in yourself. That's all."

"Does that mean the shoes weren't magic either?"

Cam laughed again. "It takes more than extra-bouncy soles to win matches! I think you'll find it's the person wearing the shoes who brings the basketball magic. *You're* the star, Zac, not them."

Zac grinned. What a relief! He sat up straighter in his seat, his chest filling with pride. He wasn't a cheat, he was a star!

"Do you mind if I keep the wristband anyway?" he asked. "To remind me to believe in myself."

"Of course," said Cam. "Now, hurry up and choose what you're having for dinner. You'll never be tall like me if you don't eat anything."

"Okay," agreed Zac. "I'll have the chicken basket meal with extra veggies." But for once he didn't care about height charts and measurements. *I might be short, but I'm still a basketball champion*, he told himself, feeling taller already.

Discussion Points

1. What does Zac want to be the most?

2. Where does Zac find the Ultra Bounce trainers?

3. What was your favourite part of the story?

4. Why do you think Zac is better at basketball when he uses the trainers and wristband?

5. Who gives Zac the lucky wristband?

a) His mum

b) Cam

c) Mrs Hoop

6. Who was your favourite character and why?

7. There were moments in the story when Zac felt he might be **cheating**. How did he deal with this?

8. What do you think happens after the end of the story?

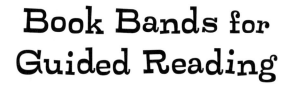

Book Bands for Guided Reading

Pink
Red
Yellow
Blue
Green
Orange
Turquoise
Purple
Gold
White
Lime
Brown
Grey

The Institute of Education book banding system is a scale of colours that reflects the various levels of reading difficulty. The bands are assigned by taking into account the content, the language style, the layout and phonics. Word, phrase and sentence level work is also taken into consideration.

The Maverick Readers Scheme is a bright, attractive range of books covering the pink to grey bands. All of these books have been book banded for guided reading to the industry standard and edited by a leading educational consultant.

To view the whole Maverick Readers scheme, visit our website at
www.maverickearlyreaders.com

Or scan the QR code to view our scheme instantly!

Maverick Chapter Readers
(From Lime to Grey Band)